Honeymooners Trivia

Mark Phillips

Writers Club Press
San Jose New York Lincoln Shanghai

Honeymooners Trivia

Writers Club Press
an imprint of iUniverse, Inc.

For information address:
iUniverse, Inc.
5220 S. 16th St., Suite 200
Lincoln, NE 68512
www.iuniverse.com

Cover illustration by Debbie Phillips

ISBN: 0-595-22084-3

Printed in the United States of America

Contents

Part 2   *Trivial but Interesting Facts*

Introduction

A story:

Once upon time a cranky but lovable bus driver named Ralph Kramden lived with his sarcastic but forgiving wife, Alice, in a rundown, grimly stark Brooklyn apartment. One flight above them lived their loyal best friends, a childlike, easygoing sewer worker named Ed Norton and his wife, Trixie. Ralph, often with the help of Norton, constantly tried to better his lot in life—sometimes through hare-brained get-rich-quick schemes, other times through sheer determination—but perpetually failed. The end.

Now, that's not much of a story. After all, most stories have a beginning, a middle, and an end, but this one has only a middle! So why don't we sketch in a beginning and end?

If the time is around the early or mid 1950s and Ralph has worked for the Gotham Bus Company for about 15 years, then he first began driving a bus immediately after the Great Depression. As a youngster, Ralph would have witnessed first-hand the 12-year economic crisis in which banks and businesses failed and millions of people lost their jobs and lived in poverty. And he couldn't have helped but taste the fear and desperation that pervaded the calamity. So who could blame him, with his limited education and paltry bus driver's wages, from looking for some kind—any kind—of insurance policy against a repetition of that miserable misfortune. Who could blame him for dreaming of striking it rich with no-cal pizza or glow-in-the-dark wallpaper?

And what kind of life did he live, anyway? Continual aggravation as a New York City bus driver all day, and then a beyond-Spartan, two-steps-below-shabby apartment at night. It's no wonder he needed evenings out with Norton shooting pool, bowling, or attending Raccoon Lodge meetings!

Now, how about an ending for our story? But, of course, there can't be one. What would you like, that one of Ralph's money-making schemes succeeded, or that he did get that big promotion at the bus company? If that were to happen, there'd be no more story—because Ralph's struggle for wealth and respectability *is* the story. Only in his struggle do we see the true Ralph. Sure, as he blusters his way through his schemes and scams, he appears grouchy at best, explosively hotheaded at worst. But all along we know that what really motivates him is an understandable fear of the squalor poverty can bring, an inherent longing to *be* somebody, and a need to provide for his wife's safety and security. And when his plans fail, his irritable expression magically changes and the real Ralph bursts forth, humble, blame-accepting, apologetic, and appreciative; in other words, a loving and lovable guy.

Now let's take a more detailed look into the life and times of this loving and lovable guy, his friends, his family, and the trials and tribulations that made him into an Everyman.

PART 1

Trivia Questions

1

Ralph

1. What is Ralph's salary?
a. $62 a week
b. $95 a week
c. $79 a week

2. How much does Ralph's doctor charge for a regular checkup?
a. $10
b. $3
c. $15

3. For which store did Ralph once deliver groceries?
a. A&P
b. Bensonhurst Deli
c. Kraus's Market

4. Why does Ralph say he doesn't want to buy a television?
a. It's too expensive
b. It isn't necessary
c. He's waiting for 3-D television

5. What is Ralph's blood type?
a. A
b. B
c. O

6. According to Ralph, where is the best place to test a cure for aggravation?
a. The bus
b. New York City
c. The subway

7. What time does Ralph leave for work in the morning?
a. 8:00 a.m.
b. 7:00 a.m.
c. 7:30 a.m.

8A. What did Ralph's uncle want Ralph to be when he grew up?
a. A doctor
b. A lawyer
c. An architect

8B. Why did Ralph give up those studies?
a. He couldn't afford them
b. To take Charleston lessons
c. He didn't have the brains

9A. When Ralph puts a list of his good and bad points on the wall, what is at the top of his list of good points?
a. Admits mistakes
b. Good bowler
c. Loves wife

9B. What is at the top of his list of bad points?
a. Late for work
b. Doesn't speak French
c. Loses temper

9C. What is fault number 18?
a. Treats wife like workhorse
b. Isn't patient
c. Thinks about money too much

9D. What is fault number 22?
a. Yells at Norton
b. Brags too much
c. Argues too much

10A. Ralph expects his income tax refund to amount to
a. $97
b. $42
c. $62

10B. He plans to spend the money on a vacation at
a. Raccoon Point
b. Adventureland
c. Fred's Landing

11A. Ralph receives a letter from the IRS asking him to report to
a. Sam Prescott
b. Richard Puder
c. Dick O'Donnell

11B. When is Ralph to report
a. 8 a.m. on the 1st
b. 9 a.m. on the 12th
c. 10 a.m. on the 21st

12. Where did Ralph win a pinball contest?
a. Salvatores's Pizzeria
b. The Raccoon Lodge
c. The bowling alley

13. What is Ralph's social security number?
a. 2804324
b. 1053622
c. 1068739

14. Ralph won five dollars at the Raccoon picnic by winning the
a. Pie eating contest
b. Three-legged race
c. Dance contest

15. What costume did Ralph wear in the 1949 Bus Driver's Frolics?
a. Ballet dress
b. Gorilla
c. Spaceman

16. When does Ralph usually get home from work?
a. 5:30 p.m.
b. 6:30 p.m.
c. 6:00 p.m.

17. According to Ralph, when he was younger, while other guys bummed around street corners and pool rooms, he spent every night of the week at
a. Roseland
b. Home
c. The bowling alley

2

Alice

1. When Alice gets a job as a secretary, who is her boss?
a. Charlie Fingers
b. Tony Amico
c. Mr. Dumont

2. For how many months did Alice give up going to the beauty parlor in order to buy her fishing equipment?
a. One
b. Two
c. Three

3. To marry Ralph, Alice gave up a job in a
a. Bakery
b. Laundry
c. Office

4. Who asks Alice if she knows a baby-sitter?
a. Mrs. Stevens
b. Mrs. Simpson
c. Mrs. Schwartz

5. Alice takes a baby-sitting job for
a. 50 cents an hour
b. 75 cents an hour
c. A dollar an hour

6A. For whom does Alice baby-sit first?
a. The Bartfells
b. The Bormans
c. The Browns

6B. What is their address?
a. 621 Kosciusko St.
b. 383 Himrod St.
c. 11 Bushwick Av.

6C. What apartment?
a. 3H
b. 5B
c. 4D

6D. How far is that from the Kramdens' building?
a. Three blocks
b. Six blocks
c. Eleven blocks

7A. Who else does Alice baby-sit for?
a. The Wolhstetters
b. The Shermans
c. The Williamses

7B. What is the father's first name?
a. Bruce
b. Frederick
c. Harvey

7C. What is the mother's first name?
a. Helen
b. Muriel
c. Myrtle

7D. What is their address?
a. 61 Bensonhurst Av.
b. 316 Flatbush Av.
c. 465 Van Buren St.

7E. What apartment?
a. 3C
b. 4D
c. 5E

7F. How long have they been married?
a. Five years
b. Ten years
c. Fifteen years

8A. Alice gets a job in a bakery so that she and Ralph can afford to pay a maid. Which bakery is it?
a. Kraus's Bakery
b. Krausmeyer's Bakery
c. Morgan's Bakery

8B. What does she do there?
a. She bakes donuts
b. She works the counter
c. She stuffs jelly into donuts

8C. To what position is she promoted?
a. Jelly donut taster
b. Assistant manager
c. Chief cashier

3

Norton

1. Whom does Norton refer to as "Madame Guillotine"?
a. His mother-in-law
b. Trixie
c. His cousin

2A. After Norton gets fired, where does he find a new job?
a. Ace Plumbing Co.
b. Spiffy Iron Co.
c. Acme Brush Co.

2B. What is his position in that company?
a. Door-to-door salesman
b. Manager
c. Clerk

2C. How much does Norton tell Ralph he made on his first day on his new job?
a. $25
b. $40
c. $100

3. In which branch of the military did Norton serve?
a. Navy
b. Army
c. Coast Guard

4. According to Norton, his cousin looks like
a. Frankenstein
b. A gorilla
c. An orangutan

5. According to Norton, if his mother-in-law went on *The $64,000 Question,* what would her category be?
a. Ugly
b. Nasty
c. Mean

6. According to Norton, in *Ring* magazine, who is the number two contender for the Marciano title?
a. His boss
b. His mother-in-law
c. His cousin

7A. Which stickball team does Norton coach?
a. The Cougars
b. The Hurricanes
c. The Bears

7B. Who is the captain?
a. Ed Norton
b. Tommy Doyal
c. Johnny Bennett

7C. What did Norton promise to give each player who hit a home run?
a. A banana
b. An apple
c. An orange

8. Norton's friend had the hiccups for three weeks. For how much did he sell his story to a magazine?
a. $500
b. $1000
c. $5000

9. When Norton poses as a doctor, where does he say he went to school?
a. P.S. 12
b. P.S. 19
c. P.S. 31

10. When Norton watches *Captain Video* at the Kramdens' apartment, Captain Video blasts off for
a. Jupiter
b. Pluto
c. Neptune

11. What is Norton's ranking in the Captain Video Space Academy?
a. Ranger 3rd class
b. Scout 2nd class
c. Explorer 4th class

12. What does Norton bump his head into while sleepwalking?
a. The fire escape ladder
b. The side of a building
c. A clothesline

13. Where does Norton sleepwalk on Thursday nights?
a. Himrod St. sewer
b. Tunnel of Love
c. Kosciusko St. sewer

14A. Norton's company doctor injects Norton with
a. Pentathol
b. A tranquilizer
c. Sleep serum

14B. After the injection Norton counts backwards from 100. How far does he get before he skips all the way down to 3?
a. 97
b. 96
c. 95

15. Why wasn't Norton admitted to college?
a. His grades were too low
b. He couldn't afford it
c. They said he had to finish grammar school first

16A. When Norton was a child, at which amusement park did he lose his dog Lulu?
a. Coney Island
b. Palisades Park
c. Rockaway Playland

16B. At which ride?
a. Roller coaster
b. Tunnel of Love
c. Tilt-a-whirl

17. In Norton's birdwatching diary he writes that he spotted two yellow-bellied sapsuckers in
a. Bismarck, North Dakota
b. Norfolk, Virginia
c. Albuquerque, New Mexico

18. Where does Norton say he heard the line about a man being the king of the castle?
a. A Charlie Chan movie
b. A Tarzan movie
c. A Robin Hood movie

19. How much does Norton weigh?
a. 150 pounds
b. 160 pounds
c. 165 pounds

20. What was Norton's old bachelor uncle's job?
a. Sewer worker
b. Night watchman
c. Brewery worker

21. Norton takes a civil service exam to get a job as a
a. Sewer inspector
b. Sewer supervisor
c. Sewer foreman

22. What does Norton play on Ralph's cornet?
a. Swanee River
b. Shuffle Off to Buffalo
c. Reveille

23A. According to Norton, who is the chef at the Waldorf?
a. Grace Kelly's father
b. Oscar
c. Pierre

23B. And who is the chef at the Ritz?
a. Grace Kelly's father
b. Oscar
c. Pierre

24. What is Norton's middle initial?
a. B
b. H
c. L

25. According to Norton, what is the "garden spot of the world"?
a. New Jersey
b. Brooklyn
c. The sewer

26. What does Norton usually do on Saturday afternoons?
a. Goes bowling with Ralph
b. Watches *Captain Video*
c. Goes shopping with Trixie

27. According to Norton, who is the ugliest woman who ever lived?
a. His mother-in-law
b. His cousin
c. His boss in the sewer

28. Where does Norton take baths when the water in his apartment isn't working?
a. Ralph's apartment
b. The Raccoon Lodge
c. Fred's Gasoline Station

29. According to Norton, who is a good lawyer specializing in eviction cases?
a. Fred Carson
b. Sam Wiggams
c. Gil Penza

30. How did Norton earn money during the depression?
a. Shoveling snow
b. Caddying
c. Cutting grass

4
Ralph and Alice

1. In which section of Brooklyn do the Kramdens live?
a. Bensonhurst
b. Bay Ridge
c. Flatbush

2. What is the Kramdens' address?
a. 712 Van Buren St.
b. 726 Himrod St.
c. 328 Chauncey St.

3. At the time Ralph is laid off at work, what is the sum total of the Kramdens bank account, war bonds, Christmas Club account, and money around the house?
a. $12.83
b. $37.52
c. $71.53

4. When Alice gets a job as a secretary, she tells her boss that Ralph is her
a. Brother
b. Neighbor
c. Husband

5. When Ralph and Alice were dating, how much did they pay for a Chinese dinner?
a. 60 cents
b. 95 cents
c. $1.25

6. How long have Ralph and Alice been married?
a. About 10 years
b. About 15 years
c. About 20 years

7A. What did Ralph call Alice when they first got married?
a. Bunny
b. Sweetums
c. Sugarplum

7B. What did Alice call Ralph?
a. Dreamboat
b. Buttercup
c. Tubby

8. When did Ralph promise to get two tickets to take Alice to a real Broadway show?
a. August 5, 1942
b. May 3, 1947
c. October 31, 1950

9. How much is the Kramdens' electric bill?
a. 39 cents
b. 89 cents
c. $1.17

10. Where was Alice when Ralph was practicing his golf swing?
a. At Trixie's
b. Shopping
c. At the movies

11. Why does Ralph flatter Alice by referring to her as "Marilyn Monroe"?
a. He wants money
b. He wants her to not attend the Raccoons' fishing trip
c. He wants to convince her to quit her job

12A. When Ralph and Alice want to hire a maid, which employment agency do they go to?
a. Star
b. Sunshine
c. Stellar

12B. Whom do they speak with at the agency?
a. Mr. Forbes
b. Mr. Wilson
c. Mr. Puder

12C. What is the name of the maid they hire?
a. Thelma
b. Gertrude
c. Shirley

12D. What are the maid's days off?
a. Sundays
b. Thursdays
c. Sundays and Thursdays

13. Ralph tells Alice that the reason she married him was because she was in love with
a. His money
b. Him
c. His uniform

14. How much do the Kramdens pay for butter?
a. 13 cents a pound
b. 29 cents a pound
c. 89 cents a pound

15A. How much money did Ralph have stashed away to use for Alice's Christmas present?
a. $15
b. $22
c. $25

15B. What did he do with that money?
a. He bought himself a bowling ball
b. He lost it playing pool
c. He spent it on dues for the Raccoon Lodge

16. What did Alice give Ralph for Christmas?
a. A bowling ball bag
b. A Davy Crockett cap
c. A pool cue

17A. For Christmas Ralph buys Alice a box to keep hairpins in. It has a secret compartment for
a. Safety pins
b. Straight pins
c. Bobby pins

17B. The box is made of
a. 2000 matches glued together
b. 1000 popsicle sticks glued together
c. 5000 toothpicks glued together

17C. It was made in
a. Hong Kong
b. Singapore
c. Japan

18. Where did Ralph and Alice hide each other's Christmas gifts?
a. In the bedroom closet
b. In the top bureau drawer
c. Under the icebox

19. Ralph tells Alice that when he was growing up he used to eat, sleep, and think
a. Pool
b. Bowling
c. Music

20. When Ralph and Alice were younger, where did they go dancing?
a. The American Legion Hall
b. The Sons of Italy Hall
c. The Elks Club

21. When Ralph returns Alice's puppy to the pound, he gives the puppy to
a. Mr. Gersch
b. Mr. Garrity
c. Mr. McGregor

22A. When Ralph and Alice were first married, where did they live?
a. With Ralph's mother
b. With Alice's parents
c. With Ralph's uncle

22B. How long did they live there?
a. One year
b. Three years
c. Six years

23. Where did Ralph and Alice have their first fight as a married couple?
a. At the wedding reception
b. On the train
c. In their honeymoon suite

24A. Alice receives a notice saying the Kramdens' rent will be increased by
a. Five percent
b. Ten percent
c. Fifteen percent

24B. How much does that amount to each month?
a. $5
b. $10
c. $15

25. Where does Alice suggest that Ralph find someone to help him prepare his tax return?
a. The barber shop
b. The bus depot
c. The bowling alley

26. How much did the Kramdens' bank account earn in interest in one year?
a. 11 cents
b. $1.59
c. $2.25

27A. To prove that he's boss of his house, Ralph makes a bet with a friend that Alice will cook dinner for them. Who is the friend?
a. Teddy Overman
b. Joe Fensterblau
c. Joe Hannigan

27B. How much did they bet?
a. $5
b. $10
c. $15

27C. At what time was Ralph's friend to arrive at the Kramdens'?
a. 6:00 p.m.
b. 6:30 p.m.
c. 7:00 p.m.

28. When the Kramdens got a telephone, who was the first person to call Ralph?
a. His boss
b. Norton
c. His mother

29. When the Kramdens have a phone, what is their number?
a. BEnsonhurst 1-7740
b. BEnsonhurst 7-4401
c. BEnsonhurst 0-7741

30A. Where did Ralph buy a vacuum cleaner for Alice?
a. A street vendor near the subway
b. Dowsers
c. Spiffy Vacuum Cleaner Co.

30B. What street is that on?
a. Van Buren St.
b. DeKalb Av.
c. Himrod St.

30C. How much did he pay for it?
a. $3.95
b. $4.95
c. $6.95

5

Ralph and Norton

1. Why couldn't Norton's friend make it to the gym on the night Ralph was supposed to fight Harvey?
a. He sprained his ankle
b. He had to work
c. He had a cold

2. According to Norton, how long ago did he and Ralph meet?
a. About 10 years ago
b. About 15 years ago
c. About 150 pounds ago

3. Ralph and Norton thought they were on a train to Minneapolis. Where was the train really headed?
a. Norfolk, Virginia
b. Raleigh, North Carolina
c. Miami, Florida

4A. What time do Ralph and Norton plan to leave on their fishing trip in order to avoid taking their wives?
a. 4:00 a.m.
b. 4:30 a.m.
c. 5:00 a.m.

4B. What time were they originally supposed to leave?
a. 6:00 a.m.
b. 7:00 a.m.
c. 8:00 a.m.

5. According to Ralph, what was Norton's only original idea?
a. Removing drawers before moving bureau
b. Knocking out a guy bigger that Harvey
c. A cereal called Pablum on Pizza

6. What song does Norton play on the harmonica as an introduction to Ralph's "apology" record?
a. Swanee River
b. The Hucklebuck
c. Reveille

7. Who examines Ralph and Norton for measles?
a. Dr. Feiffer
b. Dr. Fohlsom
c. Dr. Seymour

8A. Which boxing match do Ralph and Norton watch on TV?
a. Carmen Basilio vs. Tony DeMarco
b. Bobo Olson vs. Sugar Ray Robinson
c. Maxie Rosenbloom vs. Kingfish Levinsky

8B. What movie is on at the same time?
a. Charlie Chan
b. Rhythm on Ice
c. Rhythm Inn

9. What movie do Ralph and Norton watch on the Late Late Late Show?
a. Dead Men Tell No Tales
b. The Galloping Ghost of Mystery Gulch
c. Ready, Willing and Able

10. When Norton helped Ralph learn to play golf, what did they use for a ball?
a. Nothing
b. A pin cushion
c. A real golf ball

11. When Ralph tells Norton he won't bowl in the championship match, whom does he tell Norton to call as a replacement?
a. Schultz
b. Munsey
c. Muldoon

12. After Norton takes Ralph's temperature, what does he tell Ralph the thermometer reads?
a. 108 degrees
b. 109 degrees
c. 111 degrees

13. After the Kramdens' maid quits, how much does Norton charge to help with the housework?
a. 50 cents an hour
b. $1.00 an hour
c. $1.50 an hour

14. To prevent Norton from sleepwalking, where does Ralph hide the key to Norton's bedroom door?
a. In the top bureau drawer
b. On the top shelf of the closet
c. Under the refrigerator

15. Ralph wants to celebrate the end of Norton's sleepwalking career by drinking a glass of
a. Wine
b. Beer
c. Warm milk

16. After Ralph finds out he's not invited to Norton's party, he makes plans to go bowling with
a. Joe Rumsey
b. Joe Fensterblau
c. Teddy Overman

17. Which alley do Ralph and Norton bowl on?
a. 1
b. 2
c. 3

18A. What did Norton give Ralph for Christmas?
a. Two ties
b. A pair of bowling shoes
c. A pair of spats

18B. Where did he buy them?
a. Morgans Department Store
b. Wallace's Department Store
c. The Fat Man Shop

19. When Norton gives Ralph a dancing lesson, what record do they dance to?
a. Let's Mambo
b. The Hucklebuck
c. Shuffle Off to Buffalo

20A. How much does Norton invest in the Ralph Kramden Corporation?
a. $10
b. $20
c. $35

20B. After Norton invests, what is his position in the corporation?
a. Vice-president
b. Co-president
c. Treasurer

21. According to Norton, what act of Ralph's is a "gentlemanly thing to do"?
a. Making the bed
b. Tipping his hat
c. Making breakfast

22. What is Ralph and Norton's bowling night?
a. Thursday
b. Friday
c. Saturday

23. Norton tells Ralph he should take a civil service exam to get a job as
a. Bus Driver Supervisor
b. Dispatcher
c. Senior Clerk in Transit Authority

24. How much does Ralph owe Norton for phone calls made on Norton's phone?
a. $97.60
b. $115.20
c. $176.30

6

The Bus Company

1. Ralph thinks Bert Weedermeyer is about to get a promotion at the bus depot. What position does he think Bert will attain?
a. Driver's Supervisor
b. General Manager
c. Dispatcher

2A What is Bert Weedermeyer's wife's name?
a. Rita
b. Shirley
c. Gladys

2B. What is Bert's pet name for his wife?
a. Kitten
b. Angel
c. Cupcake

2C. What is her pet name for Bert?
a. Lover
b. Tiger
c. Twinkles

3A. What is Mr. Harper's position at the bus company?
a. Senior Clerk
b. Traffic Manager
c. General Manager

3B. Where does he play golf?
a. Golden Pines
b. Blue Spruce
c. Silver Oaks

3C. Why can't Mr. Harper's regular golf partner play?
a. He sprained his wrist
b. He had the flu
c. He was called out of town

3D. Why can't Mr. Harper play?
a. He chipped a bone in his ankle
b. He was called out of town
c. He had to work

3E. Who plays in Mr. Harper's place?
a. Mr. Muller
b. Mr. Douglas
c. Mr. Marshall

3F. What's his position in the company?
a. President
b. Vice-president
c. Treasurer

4. Who is the president of the bus company?
a. Mr. Marshall
b. Mr. Muller
c. Mr. Harper

5. Where is the bus company located?
a. 44th St. and 8th Av.
b. 48th St. and 9th Av.
c. 52nd St. and 10th Av.

6A. Who is Ralph's boss?
a. Mr. Douglas
b. Mr. Mr. Harper
c. Mr. Monahan

6B. What time does Ralph's boss go home from work?
a. 5:00 p.m.
b. 5:30 p.m.
c. 6:00 p.m.

7. Who has complete say over promotions at the bus company?
a. Mr. Muller
b. Mr. Marshall
c. Mr. Monahan

8. Why isn't Mr. Marshall happy with the new buses?
a. Bad transmissions
b. Seats are uncomfortable
c. They need too many repairs

9A. Who gave Mr. Marshall a pool table as a gift?
a. His wife
b. The bus drivers
c. His children

9B. What was the occasion?
a. Wedding anniversary
b. Birthday
c. Christmas

9C. Where does Mr. Marshall live?
a. 1133 Fifth Av.
b. 1149 Park Av.
c. 1171 Madison Av.

10. Mr. Marshall offers Norton a job as
a. Senior Clerk
b. His personal assistant
c. Bus Driver Supervisor

11. Which bus driver was laid off because his nerves couldn't take the busy route?
a. Havemeyer
b. Gruber
c. Hannigan

7

Ralph and the Bus Company

1. Which bus company does Ralph work for?
a. Brooklyn Transit
b. New York Transit
c. Gotham Bus Co.

2. How many years has Ralph worked for the bus company?
a. About five years
b. About ten years
c. About fifteen years

3A. Which bus did Ralph drive before his layoff?
a. Fifth Av.
b. Madison Av.
c. Crosstown

3B. Which bus did he drive after the layoff?
a. Fifth Av.
b. Madison Av.
c. Crosstown

4. Ralph started a rumor that he would become the bus company's new
a. Bus Driver Supervisor
b. Dispatcher
c. Assistant Traffic Manager

5A. Which bus company employee recognized the aroma of Ralph's mystery appetizer?
a. Mr. Marshall
b. Mr. Peck
c. Mr. Douglas

5B. Which employee raises dogs and verified that the mystery appetizer was really dog food?
a. Charlie
b. Teddy
c. Howie

6. Who told Mr. Marshall that Ralph is the best pool player in the company?
a. Mr. Monahan
b. Mr. Muller
c. Mr. Gordon

7. Who at the bus depot makes stale jokes about Ralph's weight?
a. Joe Fensterblau
b. Teddy Overman
c. Joe Lestig

8

The Raccoon Lodge

1. What is Norton's position in the Raccoon Lodge?
a. Treasurer
b. Secretary
c. Sergeant-at-arms

2. How much is the Raccoon Lodge's initiation fee?
a. 50 cents
b. $1.50
c. $5.00

3. An applicant for membership in the Raccoon Lodge must have resided in the United States for at least
a. Six months
b. One year
c. Three days

4. Where does Brother Andrews work?
a. The sewer
b. The bus company
c. A brewery

5. What is Brother Dribbin's job?
a. Undertaker
b. Sewer worker
c. Bus driver

6A. Who is the Grand High Exalted Mystic Ruler of the Raccoon Lodge?
a. Morris Fink
b. Herman Gruber
c. Sam Wiggams

6B. Where does he work?
a. The bus depot
b. The sewer
c. At his own law firm

7A. What color is the braid on the Raccoon uniform?
a. Gold
b. Silver
c. Red

7B. But whose uniform has a platinum braid?
a. The President
b. The Grand High Exalted Mystic Ruler
c. The Raccoon of the Year

8. Who was the former Raccoon who quit to join the Elks?
a. Joe Hannigan
b. Frank Brady
c. Joe Rumsey

9. Who gets to open the first clam at the Raccoon Lodge annual clambake?
a. The Raccoon of the Year
b. The Convention Manager
c. The President

10. Where is the Raccoon National Cemetery located?
a. Norfolk, Virginia
b. Bismarck, North Dakota
c. Astoria, New York

11. What is the full name of the Raccoon Lodge?
a. The American Society of Fellow Raccoons
b. The International Order of Friendly Raccoons
c. The National Association of Raccoon Brothers

9

Ralph and the Raccoons

1. Which office does Ralph hold in the Raccoon Lodge?
a. Treasurer
b. Convention Manager
c. None

2. How much did Ralph pay for his Raccoon jacket?
a. $5
b. $15
c. $35

3A. In the election for the Raccoon Lodge's new Convention Manager, who runs against Ralph?
a. Joe Munsey
b. Teddy Overman
c. Frank MacGillicuddy

3B. Only the executive members are entitled to vote. How many are there?
a. Five
b. Six
c. Seven

3C. In addition to Ralph and Norton, who voted for Ralph?
a. Jerry Shaw
b. Stanley Saxon
c. Freddy Muller

4. Whose car does Ralph borrow to go on the Raccoon Lodge fishing trip?
a. Joe Munsey
b. Freddy Muller
c. Jerry Shaw

5A. Which division of the Raccoon Lodge do Ralph and Norton bowl against the night before Ralph's company physical?
a. Bayonne
b. Canarsie
c. Weehawken

5B. Which tournament had that division already won?
a. Ping-pong tournament
b. Mambo contest
c. Golf tournament

6. Which bowling trophy did Ralph win after the Raccoon Lodge championship match?
a. Highest game
b. Player of the Year
c. Highest average

7. What is the name of Ralph's bowling team?
a. The Hurricanes
b. The Cougars
c. The Bensonhurst Bombers

10

Norton and Trixie

1A. What did Norton and Trixie order as an anniversary present for Ralph and Alice?
a. A new dining room set
b. A vacuum cleaner
c. A television

1B. Where did they order it?
a. Wallace's Department Store
b. Morgans Department Store
c. Bloomgardens Department Store

2. Where did Trixie sleep the night before Ralph's company physical?
a. At her sister's
b. At her mother's
c. At Alice's

3. What is the Norton's phone number?
a. BEnsonhurst 6-0098
b. BEnsonhurst 3-2701
c. BEnsonhusrt 5-6611

4A. Where did Norton and Trixie go on their honeymoon?
a. Niagara Falls
b. Staten Island
c. The Catskills

4B. How did they get there?
a. They took a bus
b. They took a train
c. They hitchhiked

5. Whom does Norton say he looked like before he started eating Trixie's cooking?
a. Cary Grant
b. Clark Gable
c. Gary Cooper

11

Neighbors and Friends

1A. Who gives Alice the same Christmas gift that Ralph planned to give?
a. Mrs. Schwartz
b. Mrs. Garrity
c. Mrs. Stevens

1B. What does Alice give her?
a. A kitchen thermometer
b. A scarf
c. A set of dishes

2. Which of the Kramdens' neighbors is in the Navy?
a. Tommy Doyal
b. Tommy Mullins
c. Wallace

3A. Who is the Kramdens' teenage neighbor who goes roller-skating and to a bop contest?
a. Judy Connors
b. Joanie Sanders
c. Betty Cooper

3B. Whom does she go with?
a. Douglas
b. Wallace
c. William

3C. How old is he?
a. Almost 17
b. Almost 18
c. Almost 19

3D. What does he call her?
a. Muffin
b. Knockout
c. Angel Cake

3E. What does she call him?
a. Atomic passion
b. Loverboy
c. Daddy-o

3F. Whom did she used to go out with?
a. Freddy
b. Steve
c. Dave

4. What is Mrs. Manicotti's first name?
a. Angelina
b. Marguerita
c. Maria

5A. Ralph runs into a childhood friend who tells Ralph he has his own manufacturing business. What's his name?
a. Brad Diamond
b. Bill Davis
c. Benny Dugan

5B. Where does he tell Ralph his headquarters are?
a. Cleveland
b. Chicago
c. Pittsburgh

5C. Where does he tell Ralph his plants are?
a. Columbus
b. Akron
c. Scranton

5D. What's his real job?
a. Door-to-door salesman
b. Sanitation worker
c. Assistant plumber

5E. Where do he and his wife have dinner with the Kramdens?
a. Hong Kong Gardens
b. The Colonnade room
c. The Waldorf

5F. What's his wife's name?
a. Sarah
b. Millie
c. Rita

6A. Who is the landlord of the Kramdens' building?
a. John Fields
b. Mr. Johnston
c. Mr. Johnson

6B. What does Norton call him?
a. Sourpuss
b. Scrooge
c. Johnny Boy

7. Which of the Kramdens' neighbors reads everyone's post cards?
a. Mrs. Schwartz
b. Mrs. Stevens
c. Mrs. Manicotti

8A. Who set the low-gas-bill record in the Kramdens' building in 1931?
a. The Collier brothers
b. The Manicottis
c. The Gunters

8B. The Kramdens broke that record with a gas bill of
a. 93 cents
b. $1.16
c. $1.47

9. Why couldn't Gladys play cards with Alice and Trixie?
a. Her husband was sick
b. Her mother came to visit
c. She went bowling

10. What was Ralph's Christmas present to the janitor of the building?
a. A tie
b. A cigar
c. $2.00

11. How much, in addition to free rent, does the janitor in the Kramdens' building make?
a. $50 a month
b. $100 a month
c. $150 a month

12

Relatives

1. What was Alice's mother's Brooklyn address?
a. 15 Himrod St.
b. 78 DeKalb Av.
c. 33 Kosciusko St.

2. According to Alice's mother, which tall, slim, handsome man used to be crazy about Alice?
a. Arthur Burnett
b. Horace Butler
c. Chester Barnes

3. Who is Alice's mother's neighbor?
a. Mrs. Stevens
b. Mrs. Findlay
c. Mrs. Young

4A. Who calls Ralph his "favorite nephew"?
a. Uncle Max
b. Uncle Leo
c. Uncle Stanley

4B. Where does he live?
a. Utica
b. Rochester
c. Albany

4C. What's his wife's name?
a. Sadie
b. Sophie
c. Sarah

4D. For Christmas he gave Ralph and Alice a gift certificate in the amount of
a. $15
b. $20
c. $25

4E. The gift certificate was for which department store?
a. Wallace's
b. Morgans
c. Bloomgardens

5. What did Alice's mother give Ralph for Christmas?
a. A tie
b. Pajamas
c. Nothing

6A. Who is Alice's sister?
a. Helen
b. Agnus
c. Shirley

6B. Which of Ralph's Lodge brothers marries her?
a. Brother Havemeyer
b. Brother Saxon
c. Brother Andrews

6C. What's his first name?
a. Joe
b. Stanley
c. Bernie

6D. Who caught the bouquet at the wedding?
a. Alice
b. Trixie
c. The bride

6E. Where do they plan to live after the honeymoon?
a. With her parents
b. With his parents
c. In their own apartment

6F. The suit Ralph wore to the wedding was rented from
a. Morgans
b. McCloud's
c. The Fat Man Shop

7. Alice's mother moved from Brooklyn to
a. Flushing
b. Jamaica
c. Astoria

8. Why does Ralph's mother come for a visit?
a. It's Christmas
b. Her husband will be away for a few days
c. To give Ralph and Alice their anniversary present

13

Let's Eat!

1A. What did Norton and Trixie have for dinner the night Trixie played cards with Mildred?
a. Chicken
b. Chopped meat
c. Lamb chops

1B. How much did Trixie pay for the food that night?
a. 39 cents a pound
b. 58 cents a pound
c. 69 cents a pound

2. A Chinese restaurant can be seen from the Kramdens' kitchen window. What time does it open?
a. 4:00 p.m.
b. 4:30 p.m.
c. 5:00 p.m.

3. According to Norton, at how many feet per second does the aroma of egg foo yung rise?
a. 180
b. 260
c. 320

4. On what date did Ralph try to get money to launch his no-cal pizza?
a. June 7, 1949
b. August 19, 1950
c. May 3, 1953

5. What did Alice make for dinner the day Norton got fired?
a. Goulash
b. Fish
c. Lasagna

6A. What will be eaten for lunch at the Raccoon fishing trip?
a. Clams
b. Egg foo yung
c. Knockwurst

6B. Who will bring it?
a. Brother Havemeyer
b. Brother Andrews
c. Brother Norton

6C. What will be drunk at the fishing trip?
a. Juice
b. Milk
c. Beer

6D. Who will bring it?
a. Brother Kramden
b. Brother Muldoon
c. Brother Dribbin

7A. Who chooses the food for the victory celebration after the championship bowling match?
a. Pete Woodruff
b. Joe Hanigan
c. Herman Gruber

7B. Which of the foods does Ralph especially like?
a. Three-variety pizza
b. Neapolitan knockwurst
c. Pig's knuckles

8. What does Norton eat while he is sleepwalking on a ledge?
a. An apple
b. An orange
c. A banana

9. What does Norton eat for dinner every Wednesday night?
a. Chicken chow mein with potato pancakes
b. Moo goo gai pan with knockwurst
c. Egg foo yung with sauerkraut

10. Where do Alice and Trixie shop for food?
a. A&P
b. Krausmeyer's
c. Kraus's

11. What do Ralph and Alice have for dinner the day a mambo dancer moves in next door?
a. Stew
b. Lasagna
c. Tuna

12. What's Ralph's favorite dessert?
a. Chocolate fudge cake
b. Apple pie
c. Strawberry ice cream

13A. Which beverage did Alice plan to serve at Ralph's surprise birthday party?
a. Milk
b. Punch
c. Coffee

13B. Which of the following desserts did Alice not plan to serve at the party?
a. Pie
b. Cake
c. Ice cream

14. What did Norton and Trixie have for dinner the night Ralph and Norton played pool at Mr. Marshall's house?
a. Meatballs and spaghetti
b. Lasagna
c. Pizza

15A. When Ralph invites a friend to dinner to prove he's the boss of his house, what main course does the friend request?
a. Roast chicken with stuffing
b. Roast beef
c. Steak

15B. What side dish?
a. Potatoes
b. Corn
c. Rice

14

Local Hangouts

1. What is the hourly rate at the pool room?
a. 35 cents
b. 50 cents
c. 65 cents

2. What is across the street from the pool room?
a. A laundromat and a pizzeria
b. A Chinese restaurant and a candy store
c. A delicatessen and a liquor store

3A. At which gym is Ralph supposed to fight Harvey?
a. Kelsey's
b. Halsey's
c. Rumsey's

3B. When is the fight to take place?
a. Thursday at 7:00 p.m.
b. Friday at 8:00 p.m.
c. Saturday at 4:00 p.m.

4. How many balls in a row is the house record at the pool room?
a. 15
b. 16
c. 17

5. What is across the street from the barber shop?
a. The pool room
b. A delicatessen
c. The Raccoon Lodge

6. Who runs the pool room?
a. Harvey
b. Harry
c. George

15

Safest Bus Driver of the Year Award

1A. Where is Ralph to receive the Safe Driver award?
a. At the Commissioner's office, City Hall
b. At the Mayor's office, City Hall
c. At the office of the president of the bus company

1B. What time is the presentation to take place?
a. 12.30 p.m.
b. 2:00 p.m.
c. 7:00 p.m.

2A. Which magazine interviews Ralph concerning his award?
a. Life
b. Universal
c. American Weekly

2B. Who is the interviewer?
a. Mr. Gersch
b. Mr. Prescott
c. Mr. Martin

3. Whose car does Ralph borrow to drive to the presentation?
a. Joe Rumsey
b. Freddy Muller
c. Joe Munsey

4A. Why couldn't the commissioner present the award to Ralph?
a. He had the flu
b. He was called out of town
c. He had to give a speech

4B. Who made the presentation instead?
a. Judge Caspar Wilson
b. Judge Niles Hayes
c. Judge Lawrence Hurdle

4C. What was the judge's middle name?
a. Ralph
b. Edward
c. Norton

4D. What was the judge's wife's name?
a. Alice
b. Helen
c. Virginia

5. On the way to the presentation, Ralph was involved in a traffic accident. What caused the accident?
a. The other driver didn't see a stop sign
b. The other driver was wearing the wrong glasses
c. Ralph forgot to make a turn signal

16

The Raccoons' Annual Costume Party

1. What is the first prize at the Raccoon Lodge annual costume party?
a. $25
b. $50
c. $100

2A. Which costume does Ralph want to rent for the party?
a. King Henry VIII
b. Julius Caesar
c. King Louis XIV

2B. How much would it cost to rent that costume?
a. $3.00
b. $8.00
c. $10.00

3. Norton rents a costume but ends up not wearing it to the party. Which costume does he rent?
a. Jacques Giradet
b. Pierre François de la Briosky
c. Emile de la Pouydesseau

4A. Ralph made an original man-from-space costume for the party. What did Norton think he was supposed to be?
a. A washing machine
b. A television
c. A Sherman tank

4B. What did the judges think he was supposed to be?
a. An automobile
b. A pinball machine
c. A clown

5. Which costume did each of the following wear to the party? (Match each capital letter with the appropriate small letter.)
A. Cassidy
B. Alice
C. Trixie
D. Pete Woodruff
a. Sailor
b. Tugboat Annie
c. Playboy of the Roaring Twenties
d. 12-year-old girl

6. Norton was late to the party because there was a sewer emergency. Which sewer was it?
a. Himrod St.
b. Kosciusko St.
c. 225th St.

17

Norton and the Sewer

1. Norton and his co-workers have several mottos. Which of the following is not one of them?
a. A slip of the lip will sink a ship
b. Water is thicker than blood
c. Time and tide wait for no man

2. How long has Norton worked in the sewer?
a. 13 years
b. 15 years
c. 17 years

3A. Who is Norton's boss?
a. Morris Fink
b. Jim McKeever
c. Nat Birnbaum

3B. What's his title?
a. Foreman
b. Supervisor
c. Manager

3C. What's his nickname?
a. Ol' Muck 'n' Mire
b. Ol' Sourpuss
c. Ol' Four-eyes

3D. How long has he worked in the sewer?
a. 18 years
b. 20 years
c. 26 years

4A. Norton was hurt when there was an explosion in the sewer at
a. Kosciusko St.
b. 125th St.
c. Himrod St.

4B. Which hospital was he taken to?
a. Bensonhurst
b. Brooklyn
c. Bushwick

4C. Which room was he in?
a. 219
b. 317
c. 410

4D. What was the nature of the injury?
a. He burned his wrist
b. A manhole cover landed on his head
c. His eardrum popped

4E. Why didn't Norton stay at the hospital overnight?
a. He wasn't badly hurt
b. He couldn't afford to
c. They were short of bed space

4F. Which doctor examined Norton?
a. Dr. Hyland
b. Dr. Morton
c. Dr. Seiffer

18

A Broadway Show

1. Which Broadway show did Ralph get free tickets for?
a. Murder Strikes Out
b. Murder on Strike
c. Murder at the Bat

2. Who gave Ralph the tickets?
a. Joe Munsey
b. His boss
c. Ed Norton

3. Where does Ralph want to have dinner after the show?
a. The Colonnade Room
b. Hong Kong Gardens
c. Salvatore's Pizzeria

4. Why doesn't Norton want to go to the show?
a. He already knows the ending
b. He and Trixie have to visit Trixie's mother
c. *Captain Video* is on TV that night

5. In the show, who is the murderer?
a. The uncle
b. The husband
c. The butler

19

A Sick Dog

1. What is Alice's mother's dog's name?
a. Lulu
b. Fifi
c. Ginger

2. What kind of dog is it?
a. Cocker spaniel
b. Collie
c. Poodle

3. How much does the veterinarian charge to examine Alice's mother's dog?
a. $3
b. $10
c. $15

4. What is his diagnosis?
a. Arterial monochromia
b. Rheumatoid arthritis
c. Bacterial endocarditis

5. What causes the condition?
a. Scratching for fleas
b. Old age
c. Poor diet

6. One of the symptoms of that condition is that the tongue turns
a. Blue
b. Yellow
c. Green

7. What is the vet's name?
a. Dr. Simpson
b. Dr. Morton
c. Dr. Calhoun

20

Six Months to Live

1. When Ralph thinks he has only six months to live, to which magazine does he try to sell his story?
a. American Weekly
b. Universal
c. Life

2. Who is the receptionist at the magazine office?
a. Sylvia
b. Dorothy
c. Shirley

3. Which story was the magazine running when Ralph first approached them with his story?
a. I Was a Mambo Dancer for the FBI
b. Davy Crockett Enters Bellevue
c. Marilyn Monroe Shovels Snow for the WPA

4. At the magazine office, Ralph tells his story to
a. Dick Gersch
b. Dick Prescott
c. Stanley Martin

5. How much does Ralph receive for his story?
a. $500
b. $2000
c. $5000

6. What did he do with the money?
a. He put it in the bank under Alice's name
b. He hid it in the top bureau drawer
c. He never cashed the check

21

Counterfeit Money

1. After Ralph found a suitcase filled with counterfeit money, a policeman came to his door asking for a donation for the annual
a. Police Boys' Club picnic
b. Children's party at the youth center
c. Police Athletic League dance

2. What was the policeman's name?
a. Officer Grogan
b. Office Cooper
c. Office Kelsey

3. How much of the counterfeit money did Ralph give him?
a. $10
b. $50
c. $100

4. What kind of motorboat did Ralph try to buy with the money?
a. One with a TV
b. One with three propellers
c. One with two telephones

5. Ralph spent $100 of the counterfeit money to have his suit taken to the cleaners. Whom did he pay?
a. Tommy Mullins
b. Tommy Doyal
c. Johnny Bennett

6. Ralph used part of the counterfeit money to hire Norton as his
a. Butler
b. Chauffeur
c. Valet

22

The Handy Housewife Helper

1. How many Handy Housewife Helpers does Ralph have for sale?
a. 500
b. 1000
c. 2000

2. They are stored in a warehouse in
a. Brooklyn
b. The Bronx
c. Queens

3. What is Ralph's cost for each Handy Housewife Helper?
a. 5 cents
b. 10 cents
c. 20 cents

4. What's his selling price?
a. 75 cents each
b. $1.00 each
c. $1.50 each

5. To advertise his Handy Housewife Helper on TV, Ralph must pay
a. $100
b. $400
c. $500

6. What is the phone number for ordering a Handy Housewife Helper?
a. BEnsonhurst 5-6698
b. BEnsonhurst 6-7791
c. BEnsonhurst 4-8307

7. Which movie was being aired on the night of the Handy Housewife Helper TV commercial?
a. Charlie Chan
b. Dick Tracy
c. Flash Gordon

23

The $99,000 Answer

1. Who is the host of the quiz show *The $99,000 Answer*?
a. Herb Norris
b. Jim Becker
c. Tony Star

2. Who is the piano player on the show?
a. Don
b. Skip
c. Jose

3A. Which contestant preceded Ralph on the show?
a. Mr. Parker
b. Mr. Irving
c. Mr. Belwin

3B. What amount did he win by answering correctly?
a. $6,000
b. $12,500
c. $49,500

3C. Who prepared his final question for that week's show?
a. Professor Walter Newman
b. Professor Lawrence Segilman
c. Professor Stanley Hooper

3D. How much time was given to answer the question?
a. 10 seconds
b. 30 seconds
c. 60 seconds

4. Where did Norton watch Ralph's first appearance on the show?
a. The pool room
b. The bowling alley
c. The Raccoon Lodge

5. How much will Ralph win if he correctly answers his first question?
a. $100
b. $500
c. $1000

6. When Ralph was a contestant on the show, he was asked to select a category from a list of how many categories?
a. 8
b. 10
c. 15

7. Of the following categories, which ones were not on that list?
a. Poetry
b. Currencies of the World
c. Presidents
d. Popular Songs
e. Show Business
f. Table Tennis
g. Women behind the Men
h. Boxing
i. History
j. General Knowledge
k. Chinese Cooking
l. Famous Quotations
m. Science and Technology
n. Bridge Builders
o. Rare Tropical Birds
p. Automobiles

24

The Inheritance

1. Which of Ralph's former passengers remembered him in her will?
a. Miriam Myers
b. Mabel Merriweather
c. Mary Monahan

2. As a stock holder in the Ralph Kramden Corporation, what percentage of Ralph's inheritance is Norton entitled to?
a. 10 percent
b. 25 percent
c. 35 percent

3. Which lawyer is handling her estate?
a. Douglas Hamilton
b. Frederick Carson
c. Sam Wiggams

4. What was her estate valued at?
a. Ten million dollars
b. Twenty million dollars
c. Forty million dollars

5. Where did the reading of the will take place?
a. Her apartment
b. Her lawyer's office
c. City Hall

6A. Which relative attended the reading of the will?
a. Her nephew
b. Her son-in-law
c. Her cousin

6B. What's his name?
a. Robert Bradley
b. Richard Burnett
c. Roy Browne

6C. What's his middle name?
a. Northrop
b. Hilliard
c. Nathaniel

6D. How much did he inherit?
a. Nothing
b. $1.00
c. $5.00

7A. Who was the butler of the deceased?
a. Herbert Bascolm
b. Norman Tweels
c. Spencer Milburn

7B. How much did he inherit?
a. Nothing
b. $25,000
c. $50,000

8A. Who was the maid of the deceased?
a. Meg O'Reilly
b. Maggy O'Brien
c. Mary O'Donnell

8B. How much did she inherit?
a. Nothing
b. $25,000
c. $50,000

25

Mambo!

1. Who is the mambo dancer who moves in next door to the Kramdens?
a. Juan Suarez
b. Jose Ricardi
c. Carlos Sanchez

2. Who used to rent that apartment?
a. Fogerty
b. Cassidy
c. Callahan

3. Which record does the mambo dancer use to teach the mambo to the women in the building?
a. Mambo All Night
b. Claves for Mambo
c. The Mambo Man

4. Who is the recording artist?
a. Johnny Little
b. Tito Rodrigues
c. Henry Shaw

5. Which neighbor first asked him to teach the women the mambo?
a. Mrs. Schwartz
b. Mrs. Manicotti
c. Mrs. Stevens

26

Redecorating

1. Which department store offered to redecorate the Kramdens' apartment for free?
a. Wallace's
b. Morgans
c. Bloomgardens

2. What was Alice shopping for when they made the offer?
a. Housewares
b. Clothing
c. Curtain material

3. Who is the department store's interior decorator?
a. Pierre
b. Andre
c. Marcel

4. What does he accidentally leave in the Kramdens' apartment?
a. A measuring tape
b. A glove
c. His briefcase

5. How long does he say it will take to redecorate?
a. One day
b. Two days
c. One week

6. What color does he plan to paint the kitchen walls?
a. Bright yellow
b. Pale green
c. White

27

The Play

1. The Raccoons put on a play in conjunction with
a. Their wives
b. The Ladies Auxiliary
c. The Elks

2. Who directs the play?
a. Mr. Bascolm
b. Mr. Faversham
c. Mr. Norris

3. Who is the big Hollywood producer who goes to see the play?
a. Henry W. Smith
b. Herbert J. Whiteside
c. James C. McKenna

4. Norton fills in for a cast member who gets the flu. Who is it?
a. Joe Rumsey
b. Joe Callahan
c. Joe Hannigan

5. What is Norton's name in the play?
a. Hamilton
b. Wayne
c. Carlton

6. What is Ralph's name in the play?
a. Stephen
b. Norman
c. Frederick

7. What is Alice's name in the play?
a. Lois
b. Nancy
c. Rachel

8. Where does the cast go to eat after the play?
a. The Colonnade Room
b. Salvatore's Pizzeria
c. Hong Kong Gardens

9. After the play Alice is offered a part in a movie. What is the part?
a. A school teacher
b. A nurse
c. A mother

28

More Questions

1. What did Herman Fatrack invent?
a. Handy Housewife Helper
b. Wrench lock
c. Wallpaper that glows in the dark

2. Who lived in the Kramdens' apartment forty years earlier?
a. Mr. and Mrs. Harvey Wohlstetter
b. Mr. and Mrs. August Gunter
c. Mr. and Mrs. Lawrence Hurdle

3. What was torn down in order to build the Chinese restaurant that can be seen from the Kramdens' bedroom window?
a. A pizzeria
b. A delicatessen
c. A laundry

4. Norton invites Ralph and Alice to Madison Square Garden to see
a. An antique show
b. an auto show
c. A dog show

5. Who are Danny, Marty, and Bibbo?
a. Bank robbers
b. Counterfeiters
c. Bullies

6A. Who is the Questioning Photographer?
a. Herb Norris
b. Richard Puder
c. Dick Prescott

6B. How often is his newspaper column run?
a. Daily
b. Weekly
c. Monthly

6C. Which of the following was not a recent question in his column?
a. Should the UN outlaw the H-bomb?
b. Which is more authentic—the Canarsie or the Weehawken style of mambo?
c. Should the FBI hire mambo dancers?

7. When Norton teaches Ralph to play golf, he uses an instruction book that is dedicated to
a. Anita
b. Shirley
c. Emily

8. Who is Ziggy?
a. A bank robber
b. A counterfeiter
c. A broker with Merrill Lynch

9. Who is Callahan?
a. A butcher
b. A plumber
c. A bus driver

10. How long have Alice and Trixie been friends?
a. 8 years
b. 11 years
c. 14 years

11. How far is the subway from the Kramdens' apartment building?
a. One block
b. Two blocks
c. Three blocks

PART 2

Trivial but Interesting Facts

29

About the Cast and Show

About Jackie Gleason (Ralph)

- Jackie Gleason's real name was Herbert John Gleason.
- He was born on February 26, 1916, in Brooklyn, NY.
- He died (of liver and colon cancer) on June 6, 1924.
- His father was an insurance clerk, who abandoned the family in 1924 (when Jackie was only eight).
- His mother was a token booth attendant in the subway.
- He once worked as daredevil driver.
- In 1954 he conceived the idea of freezing special dieters' TV dinners with the exact number of calories printed on the label.
- He won a Tony Award in 1959 for his performance in *Take Me Along*.
- He received an Academy Award nomination in 1962 for his performance as Minnesota Fats in *The Hustler* (and he later played pool against the real Minnesota Fats on television).
- He composed the *Honeymooners* theme song ("You're my Greatest Love").
- His nickname was "The Great One."
- An inscription at his grave site reads: "And Away We Go."

About Audrey Meadows (Alice)

- Audrey Meadows was born on February 8, 1926, in Wu Chang, China (her parents were missionaries).
- She died of lung cancer on February 3, 1996.
- She spoke only Chinese until she was five (when she came to the US with her family).
- She made her debut as a coloratura soprano at Carnegie Hall at the age of 16.
- She was named "TV's Most Promising Star of 1953" (by the editors of *Television* magazine).
- She won an Emmy in 1954 for Best Supporting Actress (as Alice Kramden).
- She was the first woman director of the First National Bank of Denver.
- She created the interior styling of the first-class section of Continental's DC-10s.
- She was the only cast member whose contract had a royalty clause (her brother was a lawyer).

About Art Carney (Norton)

- Art Carney was born on November 4, 1918, in Mt. Vernon, NY.
- He was wounded in World War II's D-Day "Normandy" invasion.
- He originated the role of Felix Unger (opposite Walter Matthau) in the Broadway production of *The Odd Couple* (1965).
- He won a "Best Actor" Oscar for his performance in *Harry and Tonto* (1974).

About Joyce Randolph (Trixie)

- She was born Joyce Sirola in Detroit in 1925.
- She worked with Audrey Meadows *before* the Honeymooners (in a summer-stock production of *No, No, Nanette*).
- She was named U.S.O. Woman of the Year in 1993.

About the Show

- The Honeymooners first appeared in 1951 as a sketch within DuMont's *Cavalcade of Stars.*
- Actresses Pert Kelton and Elaine Stritch originated the roles of Alice and Trixie, respectively.
- It was a regular series for only one year (the 1955–56 season).
- It was filmed before a live audience, two episodes per week.

30

About the Characters

(Some information gleaned from "lost" episodes)

About Ralph

- Ralph dropped out of school after completing the sixth grade.
- He's the manager of the Gotham Bus Company baseball team.
- He's the treasurer of the Raccoon Lodge.
- He's the chairman of the Raccoon Lodge dance committee.
- His favorite dinner is pot roast, dumplings, and sauerkraut.
- His evening schedule is as follows: Tuesday, pool; Thursday, bowling; Friday, Raccoon Lodge meeting.

About Alice

- She was a member of Girl Scout Troop 35 (Red-wing Patrol).
- She once worked as a riveter in a Navy yard.
- Her evening schedule is as follows: Tuesday, bridge with the girls.

About Norton

- His middle name is Lilywhite (his mother's maiden name).
- He has no sense of smell.
- He once kept a yo-yo going for 86 continuous hours.

About Trixie

- Her real name is Thelma.

31

About the Raccoon Lodge

The Raccoon Lodge was founded in 1907. The Raccoon toast is "Fingers to fingers, thumbs to thumbs, watch out below, here it comes!"

Members of the Raccoon Lodge

- Brother Andrews
- Brother Bowden
- Frank Brady
- Brother Carlyle
- Brother Casey
- Red Courtney
- Brother Donovan
- Brother Dribbin
- Brother Durgom
- Morris Fink (Grand High Exalted Mystic Ruler)
- Brother Flaherty
- Brother Garrity
- Brother Gavin
- Herman Gruber
- Brother Hanley
- Joe Hannigan
- Brother Havemeyer
- Brother Hurdle
- Brother Kennedy

- Ralph Kramden
- Frank MacGillicuddy
- Brother Miller
- Freddie Muller
- Eddie Mulloy
- Joe Munsey (aka Joe Rumsey)
- Brother Muldoon
- Ed Norton
- Brother Philbin
- Brother Poss
- Brother Reilly
- Brother Ruggerio
- Stanley Saxon
- Brother Schultz
- Jerry Shor
- Brother Smithers
- Brother Stevens
- Charlie Sullivan
- George Williams
- Pete Woodruff

32

About the Hurricanes

Ralph's bowling team was called the Hurricanes (or, as Ralph pronounced it, the Hurr-ee-canes).

Members

- Charlie
- Herman Gruber
- Ralph Kramden
- Freddie Muller
- Eddie Mulloy
- Ed Norton
- Schultz

33

About the Gotham Bus Company

The Gotam Bus Company was located at the corner of 9th Ave. and 48th St. in Manhattan.

Gotham Bus Company Employees

- Bradstetter
- Cassidy
- Charlie
- Clemmins
- Mr. Douglas
- Miss Evens
- Herman Fatrack
- Joe Fensterblau
- Mr. Gordon
- Harry
- Mr. Harper
- Havemeyer
- John
- Ralph Kramden
- Joe Lustig
- Mr. Marshall
- Mr. Monahan
- Freddie Muller

- Mr. Muller
- Teddy Overman
- Mr. Peck
- Pete
- Reilly
- Mr. Tebbets
- Bert Weedermeyer

34

About the Sewer

Below are Norton's co-workers. Nat Birnbaum (which happens to be comedian George Burns' real name) doesn't spell his first name with a "G."

Sewer Workers

- Nat Birnbaum
- Cassidy
- Morris Fink
- Flaherty
- Haggerty
- Jim McKeever
- Ed Norton

35

About the Neighbors

Below are some of the people who lived in Ralph and Alice's apartment building.

Neighbors

- Johnny Bennett (and family)
- Cassidy
- Judy Connors (and family)
- Tommy Doyal (and family)
- Fogarty
- Mrs. Gallagher
- Garrity (and family)
- Grogan (the cop)
- The Gunters
- Mrs. Helprin
- Mrs. Hanna
- Mr. Johnson (the landlord)
- The Kramdens
- The Manicottis
- Tommy Mullins (and family)
- The Nortons
- Mrs. Olson
- Mr. Reilly
- Carlos Sanchez
- Mrs. Schwartz
- Mrs. Stevens

36

About the Episodes (Titles and Original Broadcast Dates)

Below is a list, in chronological order, of the plot descriptions, official titles, and original broadcast dates of the "classic 39" episodes (1955–56 season).

1. **Ralph and Ed buy a TV**
    "TV or Not TV"
    October 1, 1955

2. **Ralph finds a suitcase filled with counterfeit money**
    "Funny Money"
    October 8, 1955

3. **Ralph tries to learn how to play golf**
    "The Golfer"
    October 15, 1955

4. **Ralph and Alice hire a maid**
    "A Women's Work Is Never Done"
    October 22, 1955

5. **Ralph thinks he has only six months to live and sells his story to a magazine**
    "A Matter of Life and Death"
    October 29, 1955

6. **Norton sleepwalks (searching for his childhood pet dog, Lulu)**
    "The Sleepwalker"
    November 5, 1955

7. **Ralph and Ed try to sell the Handy Housewife Helper in a TV ad**
    "Better Living Through TV"
    November 12, 1955

8. **Norton presents a ring to his boss, Jim McKeever**
    "Pal o' Mine"
    November 19, 1955

9. **Alice takes a job as a secretary and tells her boss that Ralph is her brother**
    "Brother Ralph"
    November 26, 1955

10. **Ralph expects a visit from his mother-in-law, but it's his mother who's really coming**
    "Hello, Mom"
    December 3, 1955

11. **Ralph buys a vacuum cleaner for Alice and hopes to be elected Raccoon Convention Manager at the Lodge**
    "The Deciding Vote"
    December 10, 1955

12. **Ralph and Ed don't want to take their wives along on the annual Raccoon Lodge fishing trip**
    "Something Fishy"
    December 17, 1955

13. **For Christmas, Ralph buys Alice a hairpin box made of 2,000 matches glued together**
    "'Twas the Night Before Christmas"
    December 24, 1955

14. **Ralph attends the Raccoon Lodge annual costume party as a space man**
    "The Man from Space"
    December 31, 1955

15. **Ralph insults Alice's mother, then records an "apology" record**
    "A Matter of Record"
    January 7, 1956

16. **Ralph hurts his back bowling and Uncle Leo pays a visit**
    "Oh, My Aching Back"
    January 14, 1956

17. **Alice gets a new phone and takes a job as a babysitter**
    "The Baby-sitter"
    January 21, 1956

18. **Ralph is a contestant on a quiz show, where his category is Popular Songs**
    "The $99,000 Answer"
    January 28, 1956

19. **Ralph believes he's about to inherit a "fortune" when one of his wealthy passengers dies**
"Ralph Kramden, Inc."
February 4, 1956

20. **The Kramdens and Nortons go roller skating**
"Young at Heart"
February 11, 1956

21. **What Ralph thinks is Alice's home-made appetizer is actually dog food**
"A Dog's Life"
February 18, 1956

22. **Alice's sister, Agnus, marries Ralph's Lodge brother, Stanley**
"Here Comes the Bride"
February 25, 1956

23. **A mambo dancer moves into the Kramden's apartment building**
"Mama Loves Mambo"
March 3, 1956

24. **Ralph refuses to pay a rent increase**
"Please Leave the Premises"
March 10, 1956

25. **The Kramden's apartment is to be decorated for free as a depart ment store publicity stunt**
"Pardon My Glove"
March 17, 1956

26. **Ralph finds a trumpet and is given business advice by a donut tycoon**
"Young Man with a Horn"
March 24, 1956

27. **Ralph tells the Questioning Photographer that he is boss of the family, and Ralph and Ed get drunk on grape juice**
"Head of the House"
March 31, 1956

28. **Ralph thinks his income taxes are being audited**
"The Worry Wart"
April 7, 1956

29. **Ralph witnesses a bank robbery and is pursued by the criminals**
"Trapped"
April 14, 1956

30. **Ralph believes he is to be named Raccoon of the Year (but the award goes to Norton)**
"The Loudspeaker"
April 21, 1956

31. **Ralph, Alice, and Norton perform in the Raccoon Lodge play**
"On Stage"
April 28, 1956

32. **Ralph teaches his boss to play pool and Norton is offered a job as Ralph's supervisor**
"Opportunity Knocks But…"
May 5, 1956

33. **Ralph and Ed become handcuffed to each other on a train**
"Unconventional Behavior"
May 5, 1956

34. **Ralph is to receive the Safest Bus Driver of the Year Award**
"The Safety Award"
May 19, 1956

35. **After being fired from the sewer, Norton becomes an iron sales man and claims to make $40 a day**
"Mind Your Own Business"
May 26, 1956

36. **The Kramdens and Nortons visit Bert Weedermeyer and his sexy wife**
"Alice and the Blonde"
June 2, 1956

37. **Ralph gets into a fight with a brute named Harvey**
"The Bensonhurst Bomber"
September 8, 1956

38. **Ralph becomes the janitor of his apartment building**
"Dial J for Janitor"
September 15, 1956

39. **Ralph offers to pay the check when he and Alice have dinner at an expensive restaurant with Bill Davis and his wife**
"A Man's Pride"
September 22, 1956

Answers

Chapter 1: Ralph
1-a 2-b 3-a 4-c 5-a 6-c 7-b 8A-c 8B-b 9A-c 9B-a 9C-a 9D-c
10A-b 10B-c 11A-b 11B-c 12-a 13-b 14-b 15-a 16-c 17-a

Chapter 2: Alice
1-b 2-c 3-b 4-b 5-a 6A-a 6B-b 6C-c 6D-a 7A-a 7B-c 7C-a 7D-c
7E-a 7F-b 8A-b 8B-c 8C-a

Chapter 3: Norton
1-b 2A-b 2B-a 2C-b 3-a 4-c 5-b 6-b 7A-a 7B-c 7C-b 8-c 9-c
10-b 11-a 12-a 13-c 14A-a 14B-b 15-c 16A-a 16B-b 17-c 18-c
19-c 20-b 21-a 22-c 23A-b 23B-c 24-c 25-b 26-c 27-c 28-c 29-b
30-b

Chapter 4: Ralph and Alice
1-a 2-c 3-a 4-a 5-a 6-b 7A-a 7B-b 8-a 9-a 10-c 11-c 12A-c
12B-b 12C-a 12D-c 13-c 14-c 15A-b 15B-a 16-a 17A-c 17B-a
17C-c 18-c 19-c 20-b 21-c 22A-b 22B-c 23-b 24A-c 24B-a 25-a
26-c 27A-b 27B-b 27C-a 28-b 29-c 30A-b 30B-b 30C-b

Chapter 5: Ralph and Norton
1-c 2-c 3-a 4A-a 4B-a 5-c 6-a 7-b 8A-c 8B-b 9-b 10-b 11-a 12-c
13-b 14-a 15-c 16-c 17-c 18A-c 18B-c 19-b 20A-b 20B-a 21-a
22-a 23-c 24-c

Chapter 6: The Bus Company
1-b 2A-a 2B-a 2C-c 3A-b 3B-c 3C-c 3D-a 3E-b 3F-b 4-a 5-b
6A-c 6B-c 7-a 8-a 9A-a 9B-a 9C-b 10-c 11-a

Chapter 7: Ralph and the Bus Company
1-c 2-c 3A-b 3B-c 4-c 5A-b 5B-a 6-c 7-c

Chapter 8: The Raccoon Lodge
1-c 2-b 3-a 4-c 5-a 6A-a 6B-b 7A-a 7B-c 8-b 9-a 10-b 11-b

Chapter 9: Ralph and the Raccoons
1-a 2-c 3A-c 3B-c 3c-a 4-b 5A-a 5B-b 6-b 7-a

Chapter 10: Norton and Trixie
1A-a 1B-b 2-a 3-a 4A-a 4B-c 5-b

Chapter 11: Neighbors and Friends
1A-c 1B-a 2-b 3A-a 3B-b 3C-b 3D-c 3E-a 3F-a 4-a 5A-b 5B-b
5C-b 5D-c 5E-b 5F-b 6A-c 6B-c 7-a 8A-a 8B-a 9-c 10-b 11-c

Chapter 12: Relatives
1-c 2-c 3-b 4A-b 4B-a 4C-c 4D-c 4E-a 5-b 6A-b 6B-b 6C-b
6D-c 6E-a 6F-b 7-c 8-b

Chapter 13: Let's Eat!
1A-b 1B-b 2-c 3-c 4-c 5-a 6A-c 6B-a 6C-c- 6D-b 7A-c 7B-b 8-c
9-a 10-c 11-a 12-a 13A-c 13B-a 14-b 15A-a 15B-c

Chapter 14: Local Hangouts
1-c 2-c 3A-a 3B-b 4-c 5-b 6-b

Chapter 15: Safest Bus Driver of the Year Award
1A-a 1B-a 2A-b 2B-c 3-b 4A-a 4B-c 4C-c 4D-b 5-b

Chapter 16: The Raccoons' Annual Costume Party
1-b 2A-a 2B-c 3-b 4A-c 4B-b 5A-b 5B-d 5C-a 5D-c 6-c

Chapter 17: Norton and the Sewer
1-a 2-c 3A-b 3B-a 3C-a 3D-b 4A-c 4B-c 4C-b 4D-b 4E-c 4F-c

Chapter 18: A Broadway Show
1-a 2-b 3-b 4-c 5-b

Chapter 19: A Sick Dog
1-c 2-b 3-b 4-a 5-a 6-a 7-b

Chapter 20: Six Months to Live
1-a 2-c 3-a 4-a 5-c 6-a

Chapter 21: Counterfeit Money
1-b 2-a 3-c 4-b 5-b 6-b

Chapter 22: Handy Housewife Helper
1-c 2-b 3-b 4-b 5-a 6-a 7-a

Chapter 23: The $99,000 Answer
1-a 2-c 3A-a 3B-c 3C-a 3D-a 4-b 5-a 6-b 7-c, e, h, j, m, p

Chapter 24: The Inheritance
1-c 2-c 3-b 4-c 5-a 6A-a 6B-a 6C-b 6D-b 7A-a 7B-c 8A-c 8B-b

Chapter 25: Mambo!
1-c 2-a 3-b 4-b 5-c

Chapter 26: Redecorating
1-b 2-c 3-b 4-b 5-a 6-b

Chapter 27: The Play
1-b 2-b 3-b 4-c 5-a 6-c 7-c 8-c 9-a

Chapter 28: More Questions
1-b 2-b 3-c 4-a 5-a 6A-c 6B-a 6C-c 7-c 8-b 9-b 10-c 11-c

About the Author

Mark Phillips is the Director of Publications at Cherry Lane Music. His other books include *Guitar for Dummies, The Wizard of Oz Vocabulary Builder, Sight-Sing Any Melody Instantly, Sight-Read Any Rhythm Instantly,* and *Metallica Riff by Riff.* He lives in Bayside, NY, with his wife, Debbie.

0-595-22084-3

Printed in the United States
40668LVS00006B/355